MW00873984

Table of Contents

Plant Slant

See that 95% of your food comes from a plant or a plant product.Limit animal protein in your diet to no more than one small serving per day.Favor beans, greens, yams and sweet potatoes,fruits, nuts, and seeds. Whole grains are okay too.While people in four of the five Blue Zones consume meat, they do so sparingly,using it as a celebratory food, a small side,or a way to flavor dishes.Meat is like radiation We don't know the safe level.Indeed, research suggests that 30-year-old vegetarian Adventists will likely outlive their meat eating counterparts by as many as eight years.At the same time,increasing the amount of plant-based foods in your meals has many salutary effects.In the blue zones people eat an impressive variety of garden vegetables when they are in season, and then they pickle or dry the surplus to enjoy during the off-season.The best of the best longevity foods in the Blue Zones diet are leafy greens such as spinach,kale,beet and turnip tops, chard, and collards. In Ikaria more than 75 varieties of edible greens grow like weeds;many contain ten times the polyphenols found in red wine.Studies have found that middle-aged people who consumed the equivalent of a cup of cooked greens daily were half as likely to die in the next four years as those who ate no greens.

Researchers have also found that people who consumed a quarter pound of fruit daily (about an apple) were 60% less likely to die during the next four years than those who didn't.Many oils derive from plants, and they are all preferable to animal-based fats.We cannot say that olive oil is the only healthy plant-based oil,but it is the one most often used in the Blue Zones diet.Evidence shows that olive oil consumption increases good cholesterol and lowers bad cholesterol.In Ikaria,we found that for middle-aged people about six tablespoons of olive oil daily seemed to cut the risk of dying in half.Combined with seasonal fruits and vegetables,whole grains and beans dominate Blue Zones diets and meals all year long.

How you can do it:

+ Keep your favorite fruits and vegetables on hand. Don't try to force yourself to eat ones you don't like. That may work for a while,but sooner or later it will fizzle.Try a variety of fruits and vegetables;know which ones you like, and keep your kitchen stocked with them. If you don't have access to fresh, affordable vegetables,frozen veggies are just fine.(In fact, they often have more nutrients in them since they're flash-frozen at the time of harvest rather than traveling for weeks to your local grocer's shelves).

+ Use olive oil like butter. Sauté vegetables over low heat in olive oil. You can also finish steamed or boiled vegetables by drizzling over them a little extra-virgin olive oil, which you should keep on your table.

+ Stock up on whole grains. We found that oats, barley, brown rice, and ground corn figured into Blue Zones diets around the world. Wheat did not play as big a role in these cultures, and the grains they used contained less gluten than do the modern strains of today.

+ Use whatever vegetables are going unused in your fridge to make vegetable soup by chopping them, browning them in olive oil and herbs, and adding boiling water to cover. Simmer until the vegetables are cooked and then season to taste. Freeze what you don't eat now in single or family-size containers, then serve later in the week or month when you don't have time to cook.

Notes on Protein in the Blue Zones Diet

We've all been taught that our bodies need protein for strong bones and muscle development but what's the right amount? The average American woman consumes 70 grams of protein daily, the average man more than 100 grams: Too much. The Centers for Disease Control and Prevention recommends 46 to 56 grams per day.

But quantity isn't all that matters.We also need the right kind of protein. Protein also known as amino acids comes in 21 varieties.Of those,the body can't make nine,which are called the nine "essential" amino acids because we need them and must get them from our diet.

Meat and eggs will provide all nine amino acids, while few plant food sources do. But meat and eggs also deliver fat and cholesterol, which tend to promote heart disease and cancer. So if you want to eat the Blue Zones diet and emphasize plant-based foods,how do you do it? The trick is "pairing" certain foods together. By combining the right plant foods, you will get all the essential amino acids. You'll not only meet your protein needs but also keep your calorie intake in check.

Retreat from Meat

Consume meat no more than twice a week.

Eat meat twice a week or even less in servings sized no more than two ounces cooked.Favor true free-range chicken and family-farmed pork or lamb instead of meats raised industrially.Avoid processed meats like hot dogs,luncheon meats, lor sausages.In most Blue Zones diets people ate small amounts of pork,chicken or lamb. (Adventists, the one exception, ate no meat at all.) Families traditionally slaughtered their pig or goat for festival celebrations, ate heartily and preserved the leftovers, which they would then use sparingly as fat for frying or as a condiment for flavor.Chickens roamed on the land,eating grubs and roosting freely.But chicken meat,likewise, was a rare treat savored over many meals.

Averaging out meat consumption over all Blue Zones,we found that people were eating small amounts of meat,about two ounces or less at a time, about five times per month.About once a month they splurged, usually on roasted pig or goat.Neither beef nor turkey figures significantly into the average Blue Zones diet.

Free-Range Meats

The meat people in the blue zones eat comes from free-roaming animals.These animals are not dosed with hormones,pesticides, or antibiotics and do not experience the misery of big feedlots. Goats graze continually on grasses, foliage, and herbs. Sardinian and Ikarian pigs eat kitchen scraps and forage for wild acorns and roots. These traditional husbandry practices likely produce meat with higher levels of healthy omega-3 fatty acids than the rich meat of grain-fed animals.Moreover,we're not sure if people lived longer because they ate a little bit of meat as part of the Blue Zones diet or if they thrived despite it.There are so many healthy practices blue zones people engaged in, they may have been able to get away with a little meat now and then because its deleterious effect was counterbalanced by other food and lifestyle choices.

How you can do it:

+ Learn what two ounces of meat cooked looks like: Chicken about half of a chicken breast fillet or the meat (not skin) of a chicken leg; Pork or lamb a chop or slice the size of a deck of cards before cooking.

+ Avoid bringing beef,hot dogs,luncheon meats, sausages or other processed meats into your house as these are not part of the Blue Zones diet.

+ Find plant-based substitutes for the meat Americans are used to having at the center of a meal. Try lightly sautéed tofu, drizzled with olive oil; tempeh, another soy product or black bean or chickpea cakes.

+ Designate two days a week when you eat meat or other animal-derived food and enjoy it only on those days.

+ Since restaurant meat portions are almost always four ounces or more, split meat entrées with another person or ask ahead of time for a container to take half the meat portion home for later.

Fish Is Fine

Eat up to three ounces of fish daily.

Think of three ounces as about the size of a deck of cards before it is cooked.Select fish that are common and abundant not threatened by overfishing.The Adventist Health Study 2 which has been following 96,000 Americans since 2002, found that the people who lived the longest were not vegans or meat-eaters.They were "pesco-vegetarians," or pescatarians people who ate a plant-based diet including a small portion of fish, up to once daily.In other Blue Zones diets fish was a common part of everyday meals eaten on average two to three times a week.

There are other ethical and health considerations involved in including fish in your diet.In the world's blue zones, in most cases, the fish being eaten are small, relatively inexpensive fish such as sardines, anchovies, and cod middle of the foodchain species that are not exposed to the high levels of mercury or other chemicals like PCBs that pollute our gourmet fish supply today.People in the blue zones don't overfish the waters as corporate fisheries do threatening to deplete entire species.Blue zones fishermen cannot afford to wreak havoc on the ecosystems they depend on. There is no Blue Zones diet evidence favoring any particular fish, though, including salmon.

How you can do it:

+ Learn what three ounces looks like whether it's three ounces of a larger fish such as snapper or trout or three ounces of smaller fish such as sardines or anchovies.

+ Favor mid-chain fish like trout, snapper,grouper, sardines and anchovies.To replicate a Blue Zones diet, avoid predator fish like swordfish,shark or tuna. Avoid overfished species like Chilean sea bass.

+ Steer clear of "farmed" fish, as they are typically raised in overcrowded pens that make it necessary to use antibiotics,pesticides and coloring.

Diminish Dairy

Minimize your consumption of cow's milk and dairy products such as cheese, cream, and butter.

Cow's milk does not figure significantly in any Blue Zones diet except that of the Adventists, some of whom eat eggs and dairy products. In terms of the human diet dairy is a relative newcomer, introduced about 8,000 to 10,000 years ago.Our digestive systems are not optimized for milk or milk products (other than human milk) and now we recognize that the number of people who (often unknowingly) have some difficulty digesting lactose may be as high as 60%.

Arguments against milk often focus on its high fat and sugar content.Neal Barnard the founder and president of the Physicians Committee for Responsible Medicine points out that 49% of the calories in whole milk and about 70% of the calories in cheese come from fat and that much of this fat is saturated.All milk has lactose sugar as well. About 55% of the calories in skim milk come from lactose sugar for example.

While Americans have relied on milk for calcium and protein for decades in the Blue Zones diet people get these nutrients from plant-based sources. One cup of cooked kale or two-thirds of a cup of tofu, for instance, provides just as much bioavailable calcium as a cup of milk.

Small amounts of sheep's milk or goat's milk products especially full-fat,naturally fermented yogurt with no added sugars a few times weekly are okay in a Blue Zones diet.Goat's and sheep's milk products do figure prominently in the traditional menus of both the Ikarian and Sardinian Blue Zones.

We don't know if it's the goat's milk or sheep's milk that makes people healthier or if it's the fact that people in the blue zones climb up and down the same hilly terrain as the goats.Interestingly, most goat's milk in the Blue Zones diet is consumed not as liquid but as fermented products such as yogurt, sour milk, or cheese. Although goat's milk contains lactose it also contains lactase, an enzyme that helps the body digest lactose.

How you can do it:

+ Try unsweetened soy, coconut, or almond milk as a dairy alternative.Most have as much protein as regular milk and often taste as good or better.

+ Satisfy your occasional cheese cravings with cheese made from grass-fed goats or sheep.Try Sardinian pecorino sardo or Greek feta. Both are rich, so you need only a small amount to flavor food.

Occasional Egg

Eat no more than three eggs per week.

Eggs are consumed in all five Blue Zones diets, where people eat them an average of two to four times per week.As with meat protein the egg is a side dish eaten alongside a larger portion of a whole-grain or other plant-based feature. Nicoyans fry an egg to fold into a corn tortilla with a side of beans Okinawans boil an egg in their soup. People in the Mediterranean blue zones fry an egg as a side dish with bread,almonds,and olives for breakfast.

Eggs in the Blue Zones diet come from chickens that range freely, eat a wide variety of natural foods do not receive hormones or antibiotics and produce slowly matured eggs that are naturally higher in omega-3 fatty acids.Factory-produced eggs come to maturity about twice as fast as eggs laid by breeds of chickens in the blue zones.

Eggs provide a complete protein that includes amino acids necessary for your body plus B vitamins, vitamins A, D, and E, and minerals such as selenium. Data from the Adventist Health Study 2 showed that egg-eating vegetarians lived slightly longer than vegans(though they tended to weigh more).

There are other health concerns that might influence your decision to eat eggs as part of your Blue Zones diet.Diabetics need to be cautious about consuming egg yolks and egg consumption has been correlated to higher rates of prostate cancer for men and exacerbated kidney problems for women.Academics still argue about the effect of dietary cholesterol on arteries but some people with heart or circulatory problems forgo them despite expert debate.

How you can do it:

+ Buy only small eggs from cage-free, pastured chickens.

+ Fill out a one-egg breakfast with fruit or other plant-based foods such as whole-grain porridge or bread.

+ Try substituting scrambled tofu for eggs as part of your Blue Zones diet.

+ In baking, use a Tuarter cup of applesauce, a Tuarter cup of mashed potatoes or a small banana to substitute for one egg.There are also ways to use flaxseeds or agar (extracted from algae) in recipes that call for eggs.

Daily Dose of Beans

Eat at least a half cup of cooked beans daily.

Beans are the cornerstone of every Blue Zones diet in the world:black beans in Nicoya; lentils, garbanzo, and white beans in the Mediterranean; and soybeans in Okinawa.The long-lived populations in these blue zones eat at least four times as many beans as we do, on average.One five-country study, financed by the World Health Organization, found that eating 20 grams of beans daily reduced a person's risk of dying in any given year by about 8%.The fact is,beans represent the consummate superfood in the Blue Zones diet.On average they are made up of 21% protein,77% complex carbohydrates (the kind that deliver a slow and steady energy, rather than the spike you get from refined carbohydrates like white flour), and only a few percent fat. They are also an excellent source of fiber.They're cheap and versatile, come in a variety of textures and are packed with more nutrients per gram than any other food on Earth.

Humans have eaten beans for at least 8,000 years; they're part of our culinary DNA. Even the Bible's book of Daniel (1:1-21) offers a two-week bean diet to make children healthier.The blue zones dietary average—at least a half cup per day provides most of the vitamins and minerals you need.And because beans are so hearty and satisfying, they'll likely push less healthy foods out of your diet.Moreover,the high fiber content in beans helps healthy probiotics flourish in the gut.

How you can do it:

+ Find ways to cook beans that taste good to you and your family as part of a Blue Zones diet. Centenarians in the blue zones know how to make beans taste good. If you don't have favorite recipes already, resolve to try three bean recipes over the next month.

+ Make sure your kitchen pantry has a variety of beans to prepare. Dry beans are cheapest, but canned beans are Tuicker.

When buying canned beans, be sure to read the label: The only ingredients should be beans,water,spices,and perhaps a small amount of salt.Avoid the brands with added fat or sugar.

+ Use pureed beans as a thickener to make soups creamy and protein-rich on the Blue Zones diet.

+ Make salads heartier by sprinkling cooked beans onto them. Serve hummus or black bean cakes alongside salads for added texture and appeal.

+ Keep your pantry stocked with condiments that dress up bean dishes and make them taste delicious.Mediterranean bean recipes for example usually include carrots,celery and onion, seasoned with garlic, thyme, pepper, and bay leaves.This is an easy way to mix up a Blue Zones diet.

+ When you go out to dinner,consider Mexican restaurants, which almost always serve pinto or black beans. Enhance the beans by adding rice, onions, peppers, guacamole, and hot sauce. Avoid white flour tortillas.Instead,opt for corn tortillas with which beans are consumed in Costa Rica.

Slash Sugar

Consume no more than seven added teaspoons a day.Centenarians typically eat sweets only during celebrations.Their foods have no added sugar, and they typically sweeten their tea with honey. This adds up to about seven teaspoons of sugar a day within the Blue Zones diets.The lesson to us: Enjoy cookies, candy, and bakery items only a few times a week and ideally as part of a meal.Avoid foods with added sugar.Skip any product where sugar is among the first five ingredients listed. Limit sugar added to coffee, tea, or other foods to no more than four teaspoons per day.Break the habit of snacking on sugar-heavy sweets.

Let's face it:You can't avoid sugar It occurs naturally in fruits,vegetables and even milk.But that's not the problem.Between 1970 and 2000, the amount of added sugars in the food supply rose 25%.This adds up to about 22 teaspoons of added sugar that the average American consumes daily insidious,hidden sugars mixed into sodas,yogurts,muffins and sauces.Too much sugar in our diet has been shown to suppress the immune system making it harder to fend off diseases.It also spikes insulin levels which can lead to diabetes and lower fertility make you fat, and even shorten your life.In the Blue Zones diet, people consume about the same amount of naturally occurring sugars as North Americans do, but only about a fifth as much added sugar. The key: People in the blue zones consume sugar intentionally not by habit or accident.

How you can do it:

+ Make honey your go-to sweetener for a Blue Zones diet.Granted honey spikes blood sugar levels just as sugar does but it's harder to spoon in and doesn't dissolve as well in cold liquids.So, you tend to consume it more intentionally and consume less of it.Honey is a whole food product, and some honeys like Ikarian heather honey, contain anti-inflammatory,anticancer and antimicrobial properties.

+ Avoid sugar-sweetened sodas teas and fruit drinks altogether.Sugar-sweetened soda is the single biggest source of added sugars in our diet in fact soft drink consumption may account for 50% of America's weight gain since 1970.One can of soda pop alone contains around ten teaspoons of sugar.If you must drink sodas choose diet soda or better yet seltzer or sparkling water.

+ Consume sweets as a celebratory food. People in blue zones love sweets but sweets (cookies, cakes, pies, desserts of many varieties) are almost always served as a celebratory food after a Sunday meal as part of a religious holiday or during the village festivals.In fact there are often special sweets for these special occasions.Limit desserts or treats to 100 calories.Eat just one serving a day or less.

+ Consider fruit your sweet treat in an at-home Blue Zones diet. Eat fresh fruit rather than dried fruit. Fresh fruit has more water and makes you feel fuller with fewer calories.In dried fruit, such as raisins and dates the sugars are concentrated way beyond what you would get in a typical portion of the fruit when fresh.

+ Watch out for processed foods with added sugar, particularly sauces salad dressings land ketchup.Many contain several teaspoons of added sugar.

+ Watch for low-fat products many of which are sugar-sweetened to make up for the lack of fat. Some low-fat yogurts, for instance, often contain more sugar ounce for ounce than soda pop.

+ If your sweet tooth just won't Tuit try stevia to sweeten your tea or coffee.It's not an authentic part of the Blue Zones diet of course but it's highly concentrated so it's probably better than refined sugar.

Snack On Nuts

Eat two handfuls of nuts per

A handful of nuts eTuals about two ounces which appears to be the average amount that blue zones centenarians are eating.Here's how nuts are consumed in the various Blue Zones diets: Almonds in Ikaria and Sardinia, pistachios in Nicoya and all nuts with the Adventists all nuts are good.Nut-eaters on average outlive non-nut-eaters by two to three years according to the Adventist Health Study 2.

Similarly a recent Harvard study that followed 100,000 people for 30 years found that nut-eaters have a 20% lower mortality rate than non–nut-eaters. Other studies show that diets with nuts reduce "bad" LDL cholesterol by 9% to 20%, regardless of the amount of nuts consumed or the fat level in them. Other healthful ingredients in nuts include copper,fiber,folate,vitamin E and arginine an amino acid.

How you can do it:

+ Keep nuts around your workplace for mid-morning or mid-afternoon snacks.Take small packages for travel and car trips.

+Try adding nuts or other seeds to salads and soups.

+ Stock up on a variety of nuts to include in your Blue Zones diet.The optimal mix: almonds (high in vitamin E and magnesium), peanuts (high in protein and folate, a B vitamin),Brazil nuts (high in selenium, a mineral thought to possibly protect against prostate cancer),cashews (high in magnesium) and walnuts (high in alpha-linoleic acid, the only omega-3 fat found in a plant-based food).All of these nuts will help lower your cholesterol.

+ Incorporate nuts into regular meals as a protein source.

+ Eat some nuts before a meal to reduce the overall glycemic load.

Sour on Bread

Replace common bread with sourdough or 100% whole wheat bread.

Bread has been a staple in the human diet for at least 10,000 years.In three of the five blue zones diets, it is still a staple.While not typically used for sandwiches it does make an appearance at most meals.But what people in blue zones are eating is a different food altogether from the bread that most North Americans buy.Most commercially available breads start with bleached white flour, which metabolizes quickly into sugar.White bread delivers relatively empty calories and spikes insulin levels. In fact, white bread (together with glucose) represents the standard glycemic index score of 100, against which all other foods are measured.

Refined flour is not the only problem inherent to our customary white or wheat breads Gluten,a protein gives bread its loft and texture but it also creates digestive problems for some people. Bread in the Blue Zones diet is different: either whole grain or sourdough, each with its own healthful characteristics. Breads in Ikaria and Sardinia, for example are made from a variety of 100% whole grains, including wheat,rye,and barley each of which offer a wide spectrum of nutrients, such as tryptophan an amino acid and the minerals selenium and magnesium.Whole grains all have higher levels of fiber than most commonly used wheat flours.Interestingly, too, barley was the food most highly correlated with longevity in Sardinia.Other traditional blue zones breads are made with naturally occurring bacteria called lactobacilli, which "digest" the starches and glutens while making the bread rise.The process also creates an acid the "sour" in sourdough.The result is bread with less gluten than breads labeled "gluten-free" (and about one-thousandth the amount of gluten in normal breads) with a longer shelf life and a pleasantly sour taste that most people like.Most important traditional sourdough breads consumed in Blue Zones diets actually lower the glycemic load of meals.That means they make your entire meal healthier, slower burning, easier on your pancreas, and more likely to make calories available as energy than stored as fat.

Be aware that commercial sourdough bread found in the grocery store can be very different from traditional real sourdough and thus may not have the same nutritional characteristics.If you want to buy true sourdough bread,shop from a reputable probably local bakery and ask them about their starter. A bakery that cannot answer that Tuestion is probably not making true sourdough bread and this should not be part of your Blue Zones diet.

How you can do it:

+ If you're going to eat bread, be sure it's authentic sourdough bread like the ones they make in Ikaria Sometimes called pain au levain, this slow-rising bread is made with lactobacteria as a rising agent,llnot commercial yeast.

+ Try to make sourdough bread yourself, and make it from an authentic sourdough starter.Ed Wood a fellow National Geographic writer offers some of the best information on sourdough and starters at sourdo.com.

+ Try a sprouted grain bread as part of your Blue Zones diet. When grains are sprouted, experts say, starches and proteins become easier to digest. Sprouted breads also offer more essential amino acids, minerals, and B vitamins than standard whole-grain varieties and higher amounts of usable iron. Ounce for ounce,sprouts are thought to be among the most nutritious of foods.

+ Choose whole-grain rye or pumpernickel bread over whole wheat: They have a lower glycemic index. But look at the label. Avoid rye breads that list wheat flour as their first ingredient and look for the bread that lists rye flour as the first ingredient. Most supermarket breads aren't true rye breads.

+ Choose or make breads that incorporate seeds, nuts, dried fruits, and whole grains.A whole food (see the next Blue Zones food and diet rule) like flaxseeds, adds flavor,complexity,texture and nutritional value.

+ Look for (or bake) coarse barley bread, with an average of 75% to 80% whole barley kernels.

+ In general, if you can sTueeze a slice of bread into a ball, it's the kind you should avoid. Look for heavy, dense, 100% whole-grain breads that are minimally processed.

Go Wholly Whole

Eat foods that are recognizable for what they are.Another definition of a "whole food" would be one that is made of a single ingredient,raw, cooked,ground or fermented and not highly processed. (Tofu is minimally processed, for example, while cheese doodles and frozen sausage dogs are highly processed.)

Throughout the world's blue zones and their diets, people traditionally eat the whole food.They don't throw the yolk away to make an egg-white omelet, or spin the fat out of their yogurt or juice the fiber-rich pulp out of their fruits.They also don't enrich or add extra ingredients to change the nutritional profile of their foods. Instead of vitamins or other supplements, they get everything they need from nutrient-dense, fiber-rich whole foods.And when they prepare dishes, those dishes typically contain a half dozen or so ingredients, simply blended together.

Almost all of the food consumed by centenarians in the Blue Zones diet up to 90% also grows within a ten-mile radius of their home.Food preparation is simple. They eat raw fruits and vegetables; they grind whole grains themselves and then cook them slowly.They use fermentation ancient way to make nutrients bio-available in the tofu, sourdough breadwine and pickled vegetables they eat.Eating only whole foods,people living in the blue zones rarely ingest any artificial preservatives.The foods they eat, especially the grains are digested slowly,so blood sugar doesn't spike. Nutritional scientists are only just beginning to understand how all the elements from the entire plant (rather than isolated nutrients) work together synergistically to bring forth ultimate health. There are likely many thousands of phytonutrients naturally occurring nutritional components of plants yet to be discovered.

How you can do it:

+ Shop for foods at your local farmers markets or community-supported farms.

+ Avoid factory-made foods.

+ Avoid foods wrapped in plastic.

+ Avoid food products made with more than five ingredients.

+ Avoid pre-made or ready-to-eat meals.

+ Try to eat at least three Super Blue Foods daily (listed below).You don't have to eat copious amounts of these foods but you will likely discover that these foods go far to boost your energy and sense of vitality so you'll be less likely to turn to the sugary,fatty and processed stuff that gives you the immediate and fast-fleeting fix.

11. Eat Super Blue Foods

Integrate at least three of these items into your daily Blue Zones diet to be sure you are eating plenty of whole food.

- Beans—all kinds: black beans,pinto beans, garbanzo beans,black-eyed peas,lentils.
- Greens—spinach,kale,chards,beet tops,fennel tops.
- Sweet potatoes—don't confuse with yams
- Nuts—all kinds: almonds,peanuts,walnuts, sunflower seeds,Brazil nuts,cashews.

- Olive oil—green,extra-virgin is usually the best. (Note that olive oil decomposes quickly so buy no more than a month's supply at a time).
- Oats—slow!cooking or Irish steel-cut are best
- Barley—either in soups as a hot cereal or ground in bread
- Fruits—all kinds
- Green or herbal teas
- Turmeric—as a spice or a tea

12.The Blue Zone Beverage Rules

Drink coffee for breakfast tea in the afternoon, wine at 5 p.m and water all day.Never drink soda pop, including diet soda.With very few exceptions people in blue zones drank water,coffee,tea and wine. Period (Soda pop which accounts for about half of America's sugar intake, was unknown to most blue zone centenarians)There is a strong rationale for each.

Water: Adventists explicitly recommend seven glasses of water daily.They point to studies that show that being amply hydrated facilitates blood flow and lessens the chance of a blood clot.I feel that there is an added advantage: If people are drinking water they're not drinking a sugar-laden beverage (soda,energy drinks and fruit juices) or an artificially sweetened drink many of which may be carcinogenic.

Coffee: Sardinians, Ikarians and Nicoyans all drink copious amounts of coffee.Research findings associate coffee drinking with lower rates of dementia and Parkinson's disease In addition, coffee tends to be shade grown in the world's blue zones a practice that benefits birds and the environment another example of how Blue Zones diet practices reflect care for the bigger picture.

Tea: People in all the blue zones drink tea. Okinawans nurse green tea all day long and green tea has been shown to lower the risk of heart disease and several cancers,Ikarians drink brews of rosemary, wild sage, and dandelion all herbs known to have anti-inflammatory properties.

Red Wine: People who drink in moderation tend to outlive those who don't.(This doesn't mean you should start drinking if you don't drink now) People in most blue zones drink one to three glasses of red wine per day often with a meal and with friends. Wine has actually been found to help the system absorb plant-based antioxidants so it especially complements a Blue Zones diet.These benefits may come from resveratrol,an antioxidant specific to red wine.But it may also be that a little alcohol at the end of the day reduces stress, which is good for overall health.In any case more than two to three glasses a day for women and men, respectively, show adverse health effects. For women, there is also an increase in the risk of breast cancer with more than one drink per day.

How you can do it:

+ Keep a full water bottle at your desk or place of work and by your bed.

+ Feel free to start the day with a cup of coffee.In the Blue Zones diets coffee is lightly sweetened and drunk black without cream.

+ Avoid coffee after mid-afternoon as caffeine can interfere with sleep (and incidentally,centenarians sleep an average of eight hours nightly).

+ Feel free to sip green tea all day; green tea usually contains about 25% as much caffeine as coffee and provides a steady stream of antioxidants.

+ Try a variety of herbal teas, such as rosemary, oregano, or sage.

+ Sweeten teas lightly with honey and keep them in a pitcher in the fridge for easy access in hot weather.

+ Never bring soda pop into your house.

Developing A Taste for Blue Zones Foods

If I've done my job so far, I've intrigued you with ideas on ways that you can nudge your own food choices toward those we found among people living in the blue zones. I've given you a list of foods that the world's longest-lived people eat, along with some guidelines on how to select, prepare, and eat them.But what if you and your family don't like the foods on that list even though they make up the majority of the Blue Zones diet? I could tell you all day long that broccoli and beans are good for you.But if you hate broccoli and beans, you might eat them for a while, but you'll eventually tire of them and go back to eating what you're used to.

Almost everyone is born with a taste for sweetness and an aversion for bitterness.That's because in general sweetness means calories and bitterness sometimes signifies toxins.Early humans who gravitated toward the honey and berries were more likely to survive than those who nibbled bitter tasting plants even the greens that provided vitamins,minerals and fiber which figure prominently in the Blue Zones diets today.So we're naturally going to prefer candy bars over broccoli or Brussels sprouts.

We're also born with our mother's tastes for certain foods.If our mothers ate salty foods high in saturated and trans fat while they were pregnant with us we're likely to be born with a taste for junk food.Conversely,if a woman eats a lot of garlic prior to birth the amniotic fluid will smell like garlic and the child will likely enjoy garlic.So if your mom was not a healthy eater as many mothers pregnant after 1950 weren't you were probably born with a handicap.

Finally most of our tastes are locked in at about age five.In fact the sweet spot for acTuiring new tastes is during the first year of life.Unfortunately, most new mothers don't realize this and they feed their kids porridge or sweetened baby food which inclines the children's taste toward junk food for life.Or they give in to the convenience of buying their children salty,high-fat snacks (French fries are the most commonly consumed vegetable for 15-month-olds in the United States).In blue zones, mothers feed their babies many of the same whole foods they eat rice whole grain porridge, and mashed-up fruits

Four Always, Four to Avoid

It took a long time for my team to develop the ten Blue Zones food and diet rules outlined above. And for some people they may represent too drastic a change from the foods they have been eating all their lives.I understand I was there too. When we first started working with the city of Albert

Lea,I generally ate whatever was on hand. If my kitchen was stocked with ice cream and cookies, that was what I ate.I was a stalwart follower of the "See Food Diet": See food,eat it.

I knew we needed to start with some simple guidelines.I brought together some of the smartest people I could find, and we started by figuring out how to make kitchens healthier.

We reasoned that if we could identify the four best foods from the Blue Zones diet to always have on hand, and the four worst foods to never have on hand and create a nudge we might be able to get people to eat better. I included myself among the potential benefactors.

We established a few criteria:

+ The "Always" foods had to be readily available and affordable.

+ The "Always" foods had to taste good and be versatile enough to include in most meals.

+ The "To Avoid" foods had to be highly correlated with obesity, heart disease or cancer as well as a constant temptation in the average American diet.

+ Strong evidence had to back up all food designations as "Always" and "To Avoid".

Here's what we came up with and the thinking behind each decision.

Four Always

Remembering four food groups might be an easier starting point than remembering all the foods prepared in the Blue Zones diet. Here's our list.

1. 100% Whole Wheat Bread: We figured it could be toasted in the morning and become part of a healthy sandwich at lunch. While not perhaps the perfect longevity food it could help force white breads out of the diet and be an important step toward a healthier Blue Zones diet for most Americans.

2. Nuts: We know that nut-eaters outlive those who don't eat nuts. Nuts come in a variety of flavors, and they're full of nutrients and healthy fat that satiate your appetite.The ideal snack is a two-ounce mix of nuts (about a handful).Ideally, you should keep small two-ounce packages on hand. Small Tuantities are best since the oils in nuts degrade (oxidize).Larger Tuantities can be stored in the refrigerator or freezer for a couple of months.

3. Beans: I argue that beans of every type are the world's greatest longevity

foods.They're cheap, versatile, and full of antioxidants,vitamins and fiber and they can be made to taste delicious.It's best to buy dry beans and it's easy to cook them, but low-sodium canned beans in non-BPA cans are okay too. Learn how to cook with beans and keep them on hand, and you'll make a big leap toward living longer with a Blue Zones diet.

4. Your Favorite Fruit: Buy a beautiful fruit bowl, place it in the middle of your kitchen (either the counter, center island, or table wherever gets the most traffic) and place it under a light.Research shows that we really do eat what we see, so if chips are always in plain sight, that's what we'll eat. But if there is a fruit you like and keep in plain sight all the time, you'll eat more of it and be healthier for it.Don't bother buying a fruit you think you ought to eat but really don't like.

Four to Avoid

By the same token, remembering four rules about which foods to avoid to help you Blue Zone your refrigerator and kitchen cupboard might make the process easier. We're not saying that you can never treat yourself to these foods. In fact, if you love any of these foods and they make you happier, you should absolutely indulge occasionally. But save them for celebrations or, at the very least, make sure you have to go out to get them. Just don't bring them into your home, and you'll cut many of these toxic foods that don't exist in the Blue Zones diet out of your diet without too much grief.

1. Sugar-Sweetened Beverages: Harvard's Willett has estimated that 50% of America's caloric gain is directly attributable to the empty calories and liTuefied sugar that

come in sodas and boxed juices. Would you ever put ten teaspoons of sugar on your cereal? Probably not But that's how much sugar you consume on average when you drink a 12-ounce can of soda pop.

2. Salty Snacks: We spend about $6 billion a year on potato chips—the food (not coincidentally, perhaps) most highly correlated with obesity (though fried pork rinds are closing in fast).Almost all chips and crackers deliver high doses of salt, preservatives, and highly processed grains that quickly metabolize to sugar.They've also been carefully formulated to be optimally crunchy and tasty and to deliver a sultry mouth feel. In other words, they're engineered to be irresistible. So how do you resist them? Don't have them in your home!

3. Processed Meats: A recent gold-standard epidemiology study followed more than

half a million people for decades and found that those who consumed high amounts of sausages,salami bacon,lunch meats and other highly processed meats had the highest rates of cancers and heart disease.Again the threat is twofold here. The nitrates and other preservatives used in these meat products are known carcinogens. They do the job, though and preserve the products well, which means that processed meats are readily available on the shelf at home or in the store, right there for snacking or a Tuick meal—something that doesn't happen in Blue Zones households and diets.

4. Packaged Sweets: Like salty snacks,cookies, candy bars, muffins,granola bars,and even energy bars all deliver a punch of insulin-spiking sugars. We're all genetically hardwired to crave sweets, so we instinctively want to satiate a craving by

ripping open a package of cookies and digging in.Lessons from the Blues Zones diet would tell us that if you want to bake some cookies or a cake and have it around, okay.If you want to enjoy the occasional baked treat at your corner bakery, fine.But don't stock your pantry with any wrapped sugary snacks.

How you can do it for kids:

+ Kids are naturally wary of new foods, so prepare new vegetables with a texture familiar and appealing to your child. If he or she is used to pureed foods, start by offering new vegetables that are soft or can become soft when cooked. If your child likes crispy, crunchy food then present new veggies raw.

+ Introduce new foods when kids are hungry before a meal or as a first course.

+ Do not force foods on kids. You can turn them off for life.

+ Introduce a variety of foods from the Blue Zones diet. Your kids may have a natural inclination toward peas and carrots but might hate broccoli and green beans. Serve small amounts of a half dozen vegetables at a time,a sort of Blue Zones succotash, and see which ones your kids like the best. Once you know that, you can try preparing those new favorites in different ways.

How you can do it for adults:

+ Discover what you like. Take a cue from the notes above on how kids acquire tastes and try some new vegetables when you're hungry as an appetizer before dinner, for example.

+ Learn some new cooking skills. You're not going to eat vegetables unless you know how to prepare them in appealing ways.

+ Take a vegetarian cooking class.

+ Host a Blue Zones potluck. Share the Blue Zones diet and food rules and the list of ten Super Blue Foods with a group of your friends. Ask everyone to bring a dish featuring one or some of those foods.You can all bring your culinary talents into play, trying new plant-based foods, and also use them to strengthen your social network a key goal of those who want to nudge their lives in the Blue Zones direction.

How you can do it for kids:

+ Kids are naturally wary of new foods so prepare new vegetables with a texture familiar and appealing to your child.If he or she is used to pureed foods, start by offering new vegetables that are soft or can become soft when cooked.If your child likes crispy,crunchy food then present new veggies raw.

+ Introduce new foods when kids are hungry before a meal or as a first course.

+ Do not force foods on kids. You can turn them off for life.

+ Introduce a variety of foods from the Blue Zones diet.Your kids may have a natural inclination toward peas and carrots but might hate broccoli and green beans.Serve small amounts of a half dozen vegetables at a time a sort of Blue Zones succotash and see which ones your kids like the best. Once you know that you can try preparing those new favorites in different ways.

How you can do it for adults:

+ Discover what you like. Take a cue from the notes above on how kids acTuire tastes and try some new vegetables when you're hungry as an appetizer before dinner,for example.

+ Learn some new cooking skills. You're not going to eat vegetables unless you know how to prepare them in appealing ways.

+ Take a vegetarian cooking class.

+ Host a Blue Zones potluck. Share the Blue Zones diet and food rules and the list of ten Super Blue Foods with a group of your friends. Ask everyone to bring a dish featuring one or some of those foods. You can all bring your culinary talents into play, trying new plant-based foods, and also use them to strengthen your social network—a key goal of those who want to nudge their lives in the Blue Zones direction.

How you can do it for kids:

+ Kids are naturally wary of new foods, so prepare new vegetables with a texture familiar and appealing to your child. If he or she is used to pureed foods, start by offering new vegetables that are soft or can become soft when cooked. If your child likes crispy, crunchy food then present new veggies raw.

+ Introduce new foods when kids are hungry before a meal or as a first course.

+ Do not force foods on kids. You can turn them off for life.

+ Introduce a variety of foods from the Blue Zones diet. Your kids may have a natural inclination toward peas and carrots but might hate broccoli and green beans. Serve small amounts of a half dozen vegetables at a time, a sort of Blue Zones succotash, and see which ones your kids like the best. Once you know that, you can try preparing those new favorites in different ways.

How you can do it for adults:

+ Discover what you like. Take a cue from the notes above on how kids acquire tastes and try some new vegetables when you're hungry as an appetizer before dinner, for example.

+ Learn some new cooking skills. You're not going to eat vegetables unless you know how to prepare them in appealing ways.

+ Take a vegetarian cooking class.

+ Host a Blue Zones potluck. Share the Blue Zones diet and food rules and the list of ten Super Blue Foods with a group of your friends.Ask everyone to bring a dish featuring one or some of those foods. You can all bring your culinary talents into play, trying new plant-based foods, and also use them to strengthen your social network a key goal of those who want to nudge their lives in the Blue Zones direction.

They are called blue zones,places in the world where people live longer and healthier than anywhere else on earth.Several of these blue zones exist,and in each of these places people living to 90 or even 100 years is common.And they aren't just living long either these people are living healthy without medication or disability.

Five blue zones have so far been identified and thoroughly researched by journalist Dan Buettner in a partnership with National Geographic during more than five years of on-site investigation. So what is the secret to longevity and health underlying these fascinating communities? Do they possess modern technology do they take massive amounts of supplements do they run on treadmills, do they have special genes?As you may have guessed, the answer is none of these.

The five blue zones are as follows:

* The Italian island of Sardinia

* Okinawa, Japan

* Loma Linda, California

* Costa Rica's isolated Nicoya Peninsula

* Ikaria, an isolated Greek island

Its Lifestyle, Stupid!

So lets cut to the chase instead of building up the suspense any further. After more than five years of investigation, what has Buettner discovered about why people in these places are living so long? The secret is lifestyle. Quite simply, these people live a lifestyle that includes a healthy diet, daily exercise and a low stress life that incorporates family, purpose,religion and meaning. Sure we can go into more detail and we will but at a high level it really is this simple.Although it may seem hard to achieve this lifestyle, the absolute simplicity and power of it should actually be refreshing and uplifting.People are always thinking that complicated medicine and expensive modern technological therapies are reTuired to live long and healthy.But it simply isn't so.The gift of a long and healthy life is already in the hands of each and every one of us It is up to each of us to choose the lifestyle of health and sadly most of us are choosing not to live that lifestyle.

Pollute Your Body And It Suffers Imagine That!

So lets get into a bit more detail. First off, what do we mean by a healthy diet? A healthy diet, according to mountains of literature, and now supported by blue zone investigation, is one that is loaded with vegetables,fruits,fish and nuts and low on meat, sugar, fat, and the toxic processed foods of modern civilization.Buettner actually goes into even more detail,highlighting red wine,goats milk,local teas and several other aspects of blue zone diets that seem to be beneficial Sure you can get all precise about it if you want, but my take is that the exact details, such as red wine, are not so important. What is most important is the high level theme of generally eating good stuff (fruits, veggies, fish) and cutting out the bad stuff (meat, fat, sugar).

Your body is a living biological machine.Is it surprising our bodies suffer when we stuff them with inflammatory, chemically destructive diets high in saturated fat and sugar? The literature shows that heart disease and diabetes can often be almost 100% attributed to a lifetime of obesity and poor diet. It has been documented in thousands of trials and scientific studies that the incidence and severity of several major diseases, including cancer and Alzheimer's, can be severely restricted by a healthy diet.

People in blue zones eat healthy diets, and not surprisingly they suffer from these major diseases either less freTuently or not at all. That means they live longer and healthier. According to Beuttner, in blue zone Ikaria the people suffer from one half the rate of heart disease and 20% less cancer than Americans and there are more healthy people over 90 than anywhere else in the world.

Work That Body or Watch it Wither

A daily routine of regular exercise is another theme that is common across all blue zones. Wait a minute you say I don't see treadmills and fitness centers in the remote Nicoya peninsula of Costa Rica. But that is just it! The people in blue zones don't need to artificially incorporate exercise into their lives with machines. The exercise comes for free already built into their daily lives naturally.Common across all of the blue zones is that the people climb mountains, walk through the hills,work the land and generally use their bodies in a constant grind as they perform their daily activities.And it doesn't have to be high intensity "run as fast as you can" exercise either. Often the exercise is slow and relaxed, but ongoing throughout the day.These people are using their muscles,burning calories, and circulating their blood.Their bodies are tough and healthy,conditioned by the daily routine to be fit and alert.Ready to fight disease. Quick to break down toxins and waste.

Especially in America when we see those rare individuals that actually make it to 90 years old, they are often frail and weak, hunched over in wheelchairs and propped up with countless medications Not so with the individuals in blue zones.Buettner shows us a man in his 90's who actually bests him in an arm wrestling match, and this is not just a special case.The individuals who are reaching 90 or even 100 years old in the blue zones are often able to live active, normal, medication free, mostly healthy lives all the way to the very end. Its an amazing revelation, and it gives hope to all of us that we too can live healthy in addition to living long.But to live long and healthy you have to earn it! You have to work your body everyday, or nearly so. Sit around all day and let your body turn into a low efficiency, low energy, low impact carcass and you can kiss your health goodbye.Your bones will weaken your muscles will wither,toxins and waste will accumulate use it or lose it.

A Happy Low Stress Life Now Who Doesn't Want That?

A life of low stress and filled with happiness. In theory most of us want this but in reality few are achieving it. Buettner has found that those who live long and healthy in the blue zones unanimously live low stress,happy lives enriched with strong family ties, a sense of purpose, and a healthy dose of spirituality, and plenty of sleep. Unlike the straightforwardness of eating healthy and exercising this third pillar of a healthy lifestyle is hard to precisely define.How do we measure stress? How do we measure happiness? Can one go to church once a day, once a month or not at all and still qualify as spiritual?

Although the specifics may be hard to define,I think at a high level we all should be able to grasp the point.If we are generally happy with our place in life then we behave in ways that promote longevity and health.We are more likely to take good care of our bodies and our bodies are more often flooded with hormones and chemicals associated with happiness and health.Stress is especially proven through mountains of data and studies to have serious harmful effects on the body. Cortisol, the hormone in our bodies produced in response to stress, is especially harmful to the body. Those that are living a life constantly full of stress,anger and resentment have high levels of cortisol constantly flowing in their bodies.The long term effects of this are dramatic,increasing blood pressure and generally increasing the onset and severity of heart disease and several other major diseases.

So Its Just Lifestyle Then?

Is it really that simple that the secret to longevity and healthy is nothing more than lifestyle? No magic pill is needed? No advanced machinery is needed? The answer is yes!

Living long and healthy is not mysterious.It is not hard to understand.It is a choice and sadly most people are choosing wrong If you are already living the blue zone lifestyle then good for you! Keep on doing it! If you aren't living the lifestyle, then it is never too late to start.Several studies show that dramatic improvements in longevity and health can return to an individual very soon after correcting a bad lifestyle.Living long and healthy like people in the blue zones is not achieved through shortcuts or Tuick fixes.You can't workout hard on Sunday and then sit on your butt Monday through Saturday.No You can't say you are eating healthy just because you stick a bunch of "healthy" vegetables on top of that "unhealthy" greasy pizza.You can't repent spiritually one day and expect to erase the damage of decades of stressful decisions and anger.To live long and healthy requires a constant daily lifestyle of positive enrichment for the body and mind.For many this may seem hard but it doesn't have to be,Find ways to make healthy food taste good. Find ways to make exercise a meaningful part of your daily routine rather than a burdensome chore.Surround yourself with others that share your interest in living a full life that is low in stress, happy and meaningful.Get plenty of sleep.

Made in the USA
Las Vegas, NV
05 December 2023

82153548R00046